SEA TURTLE
SCIENTIST

SEA TURTLE
SCIENTIST

by Stephen R. Swinburne

HOUGHTON MIFFLIN HARCOURT

Boston New York

All rights reserved. For information about permission to reproduce selections from
this book, write to Permissions, Houghton Mifflin Harcourt Publishing Company,
215 Park Avenue South, New York, New York 10003.

www.hmhco.com

The text of this book is set in Adobe Jenson.

The Library of Congress has cataloged the hardcover edition as follows:
Sea turtle scientist / by Stephen Swinburne.
p. cm.
1. Sea turtles—Juvenile literature. 2. Leatherback turtle—Research—
Saint Kitts and Nevis—Juvenile literature. 3. Stewart, Kimberly. I. Title.
QL666.C536S948 2013
597.92'89092—dc23
[B]
2012034045

ISBN: 978-0-547-36755-2 hardcover
ISBN: 978-0-544-58240-8 paperback

Manufactured in China
SCP 10 9 8 7 6 5 4 3 2 1
4500530676

CONTENTS

St. Kitts is a small Caribbean island ringed with picturesque bays and wild sandy beaches.

ONE IN A THOUSAND

O ne egg out of a thousand will pro-duce an adult sea turtle." So says Dr. Kimberly Stewart as she gently places the leatherback hatchling, not much larger than a match-box car, onto the black-flecked sand. Its front flippers begin to beat, heaving the tiny turtle to-ward the sea and stippling the face of the sand with miniature tracks. "This could be the one in a thousand."

Kimberly releases straggler leatherback hatchlings on Keys Beach on St. Kitts.

We are in St. Kitts, a paddle-shaped island and the larger of the two islands that comprise the Caribbean nation of the Federation of St. Kitts and Nevis. St. Kitts is about twenty-three miles long and six miles across at its widest point. Most of the interior is made up of a lush green mountain range, with Mount Liamuiga, a dormant volcano, rising to 3,792 feet, the highest point on the island. Small bays with sandy beaches ring the island.

More than sixty-five leatherback, thirty green, and fifteen hawksbill sea turtles nest on the island beaches. Kimberly Stewart came to St. Kitts in 2003 as a veterinary student to help save the sea turtles who nest there; she established — and continues to maintain — a sea turtle monitoring program.

Born in Statesboro, Georgia, in 1976, Kimberly grew up surrounded by animals on a small farm. When she was four years old,

her grandma got Kimberly her first cat from *Swap Buy and Sale,* a local call-in radio show on which listeners swap things. Kimberly's father and grandmother encouraged her to have pets and put her in charge of their goats, horses, cows, and pigs. "I loved everything related to animals," Kimberly says. "I declared my major in elementary school. I knew I was going to be a vet." Later, as a biology student in college working on a beach in Georgia, she

Opposite: Kimberly, at five years old, plays with her pet cat on her grandparents' farm in Georgia and (right) with her cat and tortoises on St. Kitts.

had the opportunity to release a baby logger-head sea turtle. "While watching that hatch-ling scramble to the ocean," says Kimberly, "I contemplated the many dangers it would face and what seemed like insurmountable odds to overcome. I began to realize my passion for sea turtles and my desire to help."

Today, Kimberly lives on St. Kitts with her two cats, a mutt named Curtis, and four Caribbean red-footed tortoises. Although she is the lone sea turtle scientist on St. Kitts, Kimberly is part of a greater scientific community. Hundreds of scientists, natural resource managers, and volunteers elsewhere in the Caribbean Sea are also engaged in sea turtle projects. This international coali-tion binds Kimberly's project with similar projects in more than forty countries. The name of this league of scientists is the Wider Caribbean Sea Turtle Conservation Network (WIDECAST), and it has inspired many of the community programs that Kimberly uses

When Kimberly was twenty-two, she had one of her first experiences with sea turtles through a St. Catherine's Island Sea Turtle Conservation program in Georgia.

in St. Kitts. WIDECAST has also developed standardized scientific methods, provided Kimberly with much of her reference library, and assisted in fundraising and training. Similarly, its research on leatherback migration and behavior forms the foundation of knowledge for younger sea turtle scientists like Kimberly. Thus, while she and her local partners, including a trusty band of volunteers, pursue the difficult work of saving leatherbacks on the remote beaches of St. Kitts, Kimberly is connected to a wonderful alliance of sea turtle people.

Throughout St. Kitts, everyone knows Kimberly by the quaint name of "the turtle lady."

Spend a week with her, though, and you realize the science of saving sea turtles is not for the faint of heart. You work nights. You are caked in sand. Beach gnats worry your eyes, ears, nose. You could sit on a biting centipede. But for Kimberly and her fellow scientists in St. Kitts and throughout the Caribbean region who devote their lives to saving sea turtles, it's all worth it. The sea turtles she studies are ancient creatures. The oldest sea turtle fossil dates back more than 110 million years to the Cretaceous period (144–65 million years ago), when the Age of Dinosaurs reached its peak.

But the modern world has proven dangerous for leatherbacks. Though they have outlasted the dinosaurs, is time running out for leatherbacks and the rest of the world's sea turtles? Are twenty-first-century pressures — a polluted and plastic-filled ocean, the loss of nesting beaches, the poaching of eggs and slaughter of adults, the risk of drowning in nets — overwhelming the marine turtle population? Kimberly is trying to find out.

Left: A leatherback hatchling stipples the wet sand with tracks and begins its life as a marine sea turtle.

Opposite: Leatherback tracks are about six feet wide. Notice the line down the middle of the track made by the sea turtle's tail.

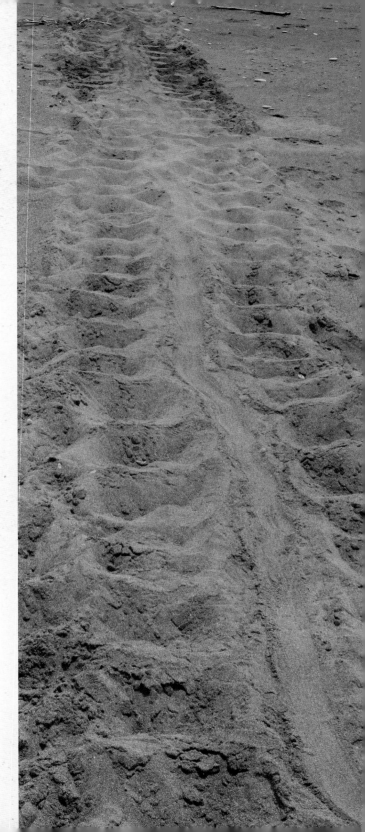

A green sea turtle nests at night, as do most sea turtles. Females generally do not nest every year, but rather every two to five years. Adults have an amazing ability to travel unerringly between preferred feeding and nesting grounds, even if these are separated by hundreds or even thousands of miles.

THE WIDER CARIBBEAN SEA TURTLE CONSERVATION NETWORK (WIDECAST)

After three decades of dialogue, capacity building, research, and community engagement on the part of WIDECAST—a network of biologists, fisheries and wildlife officers, educators, and community leaders active in more than forty countries, including St. Kitts and Nevis—75 percent of Wider Caribbean governments protect sea turtles year-round, and many of the region's most important nesting beaches are protected as well.

"It's so important that countries work together to protect the sea turtles that are left—it's all about networking, sharing what works, and making sure that people who once relied on killing sea turtles have alternative ways to feed their families," says Dr. Karen Eckert, WIDECAST's executive director. "WIDECAST's challenge is to effectively communicate to a diverse public why sea turtles are endangered and what can be done to reverse current trends."

After all, asks Karen, "What could be more threatening to a population of sea turtles than to have no one care whether they survive or not?"

In the case of sea turtles, or any endangered species, it is essential that people are motivated to take positive action. "All conservation, in my opinion, is local," says Karen, "and while this is not to say that national laws, regulations, and codes of conduct aren't essential, the truth is that sea turtles live or die every day as a result of decisions made by fishermen, coastal landowners, and others who encounter them. For a sea turtle to live another day, the person who encounters it has to live in a world where it makes sense to watch a hundred pounds of meat swim away. If people are hungry, that world doesn't exist for them, and the sea turtle dies. Voting for the survival of sea turtles is

Map of St. Kitts and Nevis, surrounded by the Caribbean Sea.

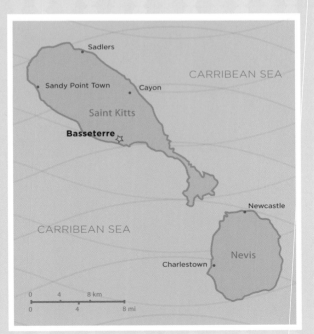

Diagram of leatherback sea turtle showing the carapace, plastron, eye, beak, flippers, tail, ridges, and pink spot.

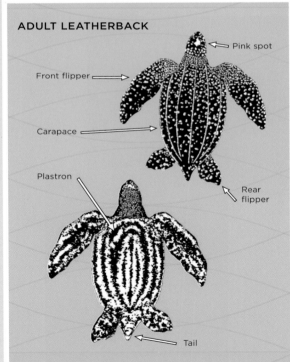

voting for the compassionate treatment of people, and recognizing that solutions to the problems we face are complex and sometimes not even known yet . . . but if we keep thinking, keep helping, and keep educating, sea turtles have a much better chance of survival. And so do we."

WIDECAST is rooted in the belief that conservation must be nurtured from within; it cannot be commanded from outside. Beyond supporting local and national efforts, like Kimberly's work in St. Kitts, WIDECAST works to integrate these efforts into a collective regional response to a common problem—the disappearance of sea turtles. Most Caribbean nations have now adopted a national sea turtle management plan, which includes dramatically reducing or eliminating poaching and illegal product sales, monitoring many of the region's largest breeding colonies on an annual basis, increasing the availability of alternative livelihood models for rural areas, and mobilizing citizens in support of conservation action.

WIDECAST helps people work together to realize a future where all inhabitants of the Wider Caribbean Region, human and sea turtle alike, can live together in balance.

A female leatherback turtle crawls to the edge of the dune to make her body pit and dig her nesting cavity.

CHAPTER 1

MEET THE LEATHERBACK SEA TURTLE

It is closing in on midnight in late May and everyone has walked a half-mile of beach along the noisy Caribbean surf searching for tracks. Kimberly is accompanied by two of her graduate students. Three local Kittitians and two American guests fill out the turtle party. Suddenly, a dark swath of disturbed sand emerges out of the surf line running straight up to the dunes. Kimberly trains a beam from her red headlamp. "It's a nesting leatherback!"

A leatherback sea turtle crawls up to the high-tide line to make a body pit and then dig a hole for her approximately 100 to 140 eggs.

A high tide washed out this leatherback sea turtle nest in Trinidad.

The 800-pound leatherback sea turtle crawls to the soft sand of the upper beach. She shimmers as the last of the seawater runs off her huge frame. Facing away from the sea, the female leatherback uses her three-foot-long front flippers to throw sand. Her strokes are powerful. As she pushes and hurls sand, her body, seven feet (213 centimeters) long, slowly rotates and settles into a wide body pit.

When the body cavity is dug, her rear flippers begin to excavate a nest cavity. The body cavity, or body pit, is a depression the female makes before she digs the two-feet-deep nest cavity or hole. She does everything by feel. She works one flipper at a time, reaching behind her, scooping out the sand, and flicking it to the side. Leatherback rear flippers are the size of a baseball glove. Imagine digging a hole with a baseball glove! Not easy. Her flippers are a multitool, though: they dig, scoop, pat, fling, and tamp down the sand.

"This area receives a very high tide in July," says Kimberly, scanning the dark beach. "We've got to relocate her eggs." Kimberly knows that sea turtle eggs laid in May will need to incubate for sixty days, so July's high tides could wash away this nest. But the leatherback still has work to do before she actually lays her eggs.

She falls into a steady rhythm: the right flipper digs, scoops, flings, tamps; the left flipper digs, scoops, flings, tamps; repeat. When her flippers have dug a hole about 28 inches (72 centimeters) deep, they begin to widen the bottom, making a vaselike nest.

Once her flippers have reached as far as they can go, the female leatherback stops digging. She pauses and rests one flipper on a pile of sand. She uses the other to shield the nest cavity, like a curtain screening a stage, protecting the nest from the view of predators.

"Quick! She's about to drop eggs! Someone count, someone get a bag!" The urgent commands come from Kimberly.

The mother turtle is moving fast now that her hole is dug. Wet, gleaming white eggs the size of billiard balls fall into the sandy nest before a bag can be set beneath her. We hear deep reptilian breaths.

"One, two, three," says Neil, the spouse of a veterinary student from the nearby Ross University School of Veterinary Medicine.

With the help of Theophilus Taylor, a towering fisherman from St. Kitts, Kimberly tucks a cloth laundry bag in the nest hole.

Kimberly spreads the opening of the bag wide as two turtle eggs plop inside.

"Five," says Neil, continuing the count, holding back the turtle's protective flipper to peer inside the nest cavity.

The rest of the group eases up alongside the turtle. They surround the nesting female and begin to collect data.

"Turtles go into a sort of trance once they start laying eggs," says Kimberly, "so we are able to work all around her. But we have to remember, even though she is incredibly focused on what she is doing, she is still susceptible to disturbance." Sea turtles spend 99 percent or more of their time in the ocean, hidden from human eyes. Scientists have an incredibly narrow but wonderful window to study them when they come out of the water to nest.

While she is laying, we walk to the front of the sea turtle and take note of her color. Her carapace, or top shell, is dark gray, almost black. Pinkish-white spots run the length of her shell and spill over onto her leathery flippers and face. Kimberly says her plastron, or bottom shell, is pale with gray-black markings. We squat beside her face.

Her eyes leak tears and mucus, pushing salt to the surface from a pair of hard-working glands in her head. Sea turtles ingest plenty of salt water when they devour their prey. Think about a leatherback consuming a lion's mane jellyfish that is seven feet wide with tentacles 150 feet long, and mostly made up of seawater. That's enough salt to cause dehydration. So salt or lacrimal glands, located near their eyes, allow leatherbacks to rid their bodies of salt by secreting saline tears.

Local islanders, though, say the sea turtle cries because she will never see her babies. Female sea turtles cannot stay out of the water for sixty days and wait while their eggs hatch. Survival for them means returning to the ocean as soon as they can or they will die in the baking heat of the midday sun. But the mother turtle is doing what she can to ensure the survival of her precious eggs. She has carefully dug a nest and will soon camouflage it.

SEA TURTLE FACTS

Sea turtles have two front flippers and two rear flippers. The front flippers help to lift and propel the sea turtle through the water. The rear flippers help steer the turtle and are used in nest digging. Unlike tortoises and land turtles, sea turtles cannot retract their heads (or limbs) into their shell. They have no teeth and instead use a large beak for crushing, biting, and scraping their food. Scientists don't know how long sea turtles live, but they estimate a lifespan of at least sixty years.

Sea turtles do not have external ears (the ear canals are covered by skin), and they are very sensitive to low-frequency sounds up to about 1,000 hertz (sounds that travel a thousand times per second). They have a keen sense of smell, often detecting prey in murky water.

Shell length of adult sea turtles ranges from about 27 to 80 inches or more (70 to more than 210 centimeters), depending on the species, with leatherbacks being the largest. Adult females can be weighed when they come ashore to nest, and scientists report weights of 315 to 1,247 pounds (143–567 kilograms) on the nesting beaches of the southern Caribbean (Trinidad and French Guiana).

The largest leatherback on record was a male weighing 2,015 pounds (916 kilograms) who was caught and died in a fisherman's net.

Color varies among sea turtles and is typically related to their habitat. Leatherbacks, for example, blend into the sun-dappled waters of the deep ocean with a dark body (black to charcoal gray) splotched with pale white, pink, or bluish markings. The plastron, or bottom shell, is pale with white to gray or black markings.

Weighing a leatherback takes plenty of muscle power.

PIT TAGGING LEATHERBACKS

Nesting leatherbacks leave behind their eggs but take something back to the sea with them. "We tag all of our leatherbacks with PIT [passive integrated transponder] tags," says Kimberly. "They are cylindrical, about the size of a grain of rice, and are encapsulated in glass so they remain inert within the body."

Kimberly and other researchers inject the PIT tags into the shoulder muscle. For consistency they place them in the right shoulder unless there is significant injury there. When a specialized reader is passed over the tag, the reader generates a low-energy radio signal that energizes the tag to transmit its unique number. The turtle feels nothing as the reader (scanner) is passed over it. The received number, an alphanumeric code with nine to fifteen characters (a combination of numbers and letters), is displayed in the reader's viewing window.

"This number allows us to keep track of the sea turtle," says Kimberly. "The tags stay with the animal for life and are very rarely lost. For this reason they are better in many ways than external flipper tags to mark and identify individual sea turtles."

A hand-held scanner is passed over the injected tag to reveal a unique identifying number for the sea turtle.

PIT tags are the size of a grain of rice but allow scientists to identify sea turtles for years.

Jon, a graduate student, flicks a measuring tape across the sea turtle's carapace. "Width, 126 centimeters," he says.

Theophilus reclines in the sand, recording the turtle's width and other vital statistics on the data card in the glow of his red lamp. The researchers wear red headlamps because sea turtles are less sensitive to red light.

"She's already been tagged," says Kimberly, holding a metal tag attached to the trailing edge of the turtle's flipper. "We'll record the tag number and check out her past nesting records." Researchers later learn from the computer records that this is the female's sixth trip this year to lay eggs on the tropical beaches of St. Kitts.

Female leatherbacks might nest anywhere from four to twelve times during a summer season. While mating between leatherback turtles has rarely been seen, females typically mate with a number of male sea turtles during the weeks prior to the nesting season, and then store the sperm until it is time to fertilize their clutches of eggs. Males play no part in nesting.

Kimberly preps the female's left flipper in order to take a blood sample. She swabs it clean of sand with an antiseptic solution and alcohol to destroy any germs or bacteria in the wound. Everyone is wearing protective latex surgical gloves. No one wants to transmit any germs to the nesting female or contract any bacteria from her.

"She's beginning to lay yolkless eggs," says Neil. Leatherbacks lay between seventy and ninety yolked eggs, followed by thirty to fifty yolkless eggs. Yolkless, or "false," eggs are laid on top of the fertile ones and are an indication that laying is coming to an end. Because there is no yolk, there is no nourishment for an embryo and no hatchling will result.

Yolkless eggs range from marble size to golf-ball size. Leatherback sea turtles are the only species to lay 30 percent or more of

Kimberly points out the pink spot on top of the leatherback's head. "It's believed this two-by-two-inch pinkish area is related to the turtle's navigational abilities," she says.

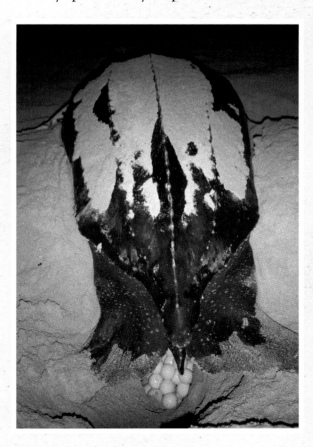

A leatherback fills the nest cavity to the brim with two-inch leathery eggs.

their clutch in yolkless eggs. Scientists are not exactly clear about the purpose of the yolkless eggs, but many believe that they provide space and aeration in the nesting cavity. The yolkless eggs deflate as incubation progresses, giving the newly hatched sea turtles a little more "wiggle room" as they prepare to emerge from the nest. When turtle researchers have to move a leatherback nest, they always make sure that they place the yolkless eggs on top of the others.

When the leatherback completes her egg laying, she pauses for a moment. An intense and long period of nest covering and camouflaging is about to begin.

"Final count," says Neil, "Seventy fertile, sixty-two yolkless."

As Theophilus pulls the bag full of eggs clear from the hole, Neil leans in and retrieves three eggs left behind in the sandy pit.

"She's covering," calls Kimberly. The research team members gather their equipment and back away. The leatherback spends forty-five minutes shoving, throwing, pushing, and tamping the sand dune around the empty nest cavity. Kimberly says you would be hard pressed to find the nest cavity after the tides have washed away the mother turtle's trail and all traces of the nest vanish.

When it seems she has tamped down an area ten times her size, the exhausted turtle finally turns back to the sea. Behind her is a set of wide tracks that marks her return trip to the ocean's edge.

As the leatherback disappears in the foam of the surf, she leaves behind her precious clutch of eggs. She doesn't know that the odds are stacked against her and her kind.

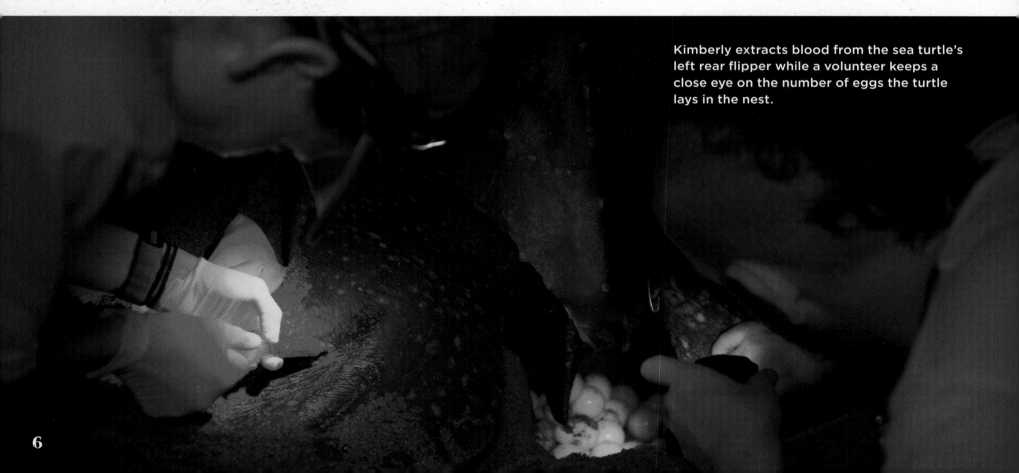

Kimberly extracts blood from the sea turtle's left rear flipper while a volunteer keeps a close eye on the number of eggs the turtle lays in the nest.

THE CRITICALLY ENDANGERED LEATHERBACK SEA TURTLE

Adult leatherbacks are the largest reptile on earth today. They dive more deeply (to four thousand feet or more) and travel more widely than any other reptile. Their range extends from the Arctic Circle south to Antarctica, and they swim, on average, about 6,215 miles (10,000 kilometers) each year. They are built for high-seas travel with a streamlined body and long, powerful front flippers for propulsion. Their smooth, leatherlike carapace gives them a perfect hydrodynamic form. As late as 1980, scientists still knew very little about this elusive species—and Kimberly's work is filling important gaps.

The leatherback is classified as a "critically endangered species," meaning that its global population has dropped by more than 80 percent in the last three generations (about a hundred years). Beaches on the Pacific coast of Mexico, for example, which once hosted tens of thousands of nesting females, now receive only a few

hundred leatherbacks nesting each year. The bad news is that humans caused this problem. The good news is that we can help to fix it.

Why bother saving sea turtles? Someone might say, "I don't miss the dinosaurs; why will I miss the sea turtles?"

Consider that without the leatherback sea turtle, a major jellyfish consumer, jellyfish populations would explode. Jellyfish eat plankton and fish larvae. An exploding jellyfish population means fewer plankton and fish larvae. Scientists worry that the outcome of this scenario will be fewer larger fish for fishermen to catch. "As is true for all sea turtle species, the ecological role

"A leatherback is incredibly focused during egg laying on the beach," says Kimberly.

of the leatherback is complex," says Dr. Karen Eckert, executive director of WIDECAST. "For the oceans to remain in balance, top predators such as the leatherback sea turtle are very much needed. As large predators become scarce or disappear, food webs, including those that contribute to human diets, become unstable. In this case, the key to avoiding dangerous imbalances is to rebuild depleted sea turtle populations."

Hatchlings make their way to the sea.

A green sea turtle grazes on seagrass. "Green turtles" are not actually green, at least on the outside. They were given this name because their body fat absorbs chlorophyll (the pigment that makes grass green) and thus they are greenish in hue on the inside.

CHAPTER 2

LAS TORTUGAS: A HISTORY OF THE SEA TURTLE

Humans are newcomers to Earth, compared to sea turtles. While most biologists estimate that the ancestors of modern human beings appeared on the planet around two hundred thousand years ago, sea turtles and their ancestors swam when dinosaurs trudged the earth, more than 100 million years ago.

In November 1914, George R. Wieland, a paleobiologist at Yale University, stood beside the skeleton of an ancient sea turtle called Archelon. The creature Archelon (from the Greek, meaning "ruler turtle") lived around seventy million years ago, when dinosaurs ruled the land.

Only seven species of sea turtle still swim in the oceans of the world. They are the loggerhead, green, hawksbill, Kemp's ridley, olive ridley, flatback, and leatherback turtles.

The ocean was once home to millions upon millions of sea turtles. Over the last five hundred years sea turtle populations have

plummeted. Today, all seven species are either threatened or endangered. If we do not reach out to help save them, one or all species of marine turtle could go extinct.

Archaeologists have found sea turtle bones in Caribbean middens (ancient trash piles) dating back more than a thousand years. Although early peoples, such as the Arawak and Carib tribes, hunted sea turtles for food, the pressure on turtle populations was most likely relatively small. When native peoples killed a sea turtle, they used every part of it — the flesh for food, the fat for cooking oil, the skin for leather, and the shell for adornments, tools, even baby cradles. The meat and eggs were considered an important source of protein in the island diet.

It wasn't until the Spanish explorers arrived in the Americas during the 1400s that the fate of sea turtles would be changed forever. Imagine yourself as one of these explorers, sighting land for the first time in five weeks since departing Spain. You sail your ship close to the island and realize that the sea is filled with moving rocks. They are sea turtles. So many that you'd think you could step out and walk to shore on their shells!

WIDECAST's portrait gallery of the six sea turtle species found in the Caribbean. Most scientists recognize seven species of sea turtle. The flatback sea turtle nests only in Australia.

Leatherback Turtle (*Dermochelys coriacea*)

Loggerhead Turtle (*Caretta caretta*)

Hawksbill Turtle (*Eretmochelys imbricata*)

Green Turtle (*Chelonia mydas*)

Kemp's Ridley Turtle (*Lepidochelys kempii*)

Olive Ridley Turtle (*Lepidochelys olivacea*)

WIDECAST
Wider Caribbean Sea Turtle Conservation Network

UNEP

These confiscated hawksbill items were made from slaughtered sea turtles.

Native people flipped green sea turtles over with long sticks before butchering them.

When Christopher Columbus landed in the Cayman Islands in 1503, he called them Las Tortugas, the Spanish word for "turtle."

A priest named Andres Bernaldez accompanied Columbus on his second voyage to the New World. As they passed tropical sandy beaches, he described the multitude of turtles: "Throughout that voyage they saw that there were many turtles and very large. But in those

A female sea turtle with eggs is harvested along a Caribbean beach. Sea turtles still provide an important source of protein for coastal people.

20 leagues, they saw very many more, for the sea was all thick with them, and they were of the very largest, so numerous that it seemed that the ships would run aground on them and were as if bathing in them."

Spain dominated the early colonization of the Caribbean islands. From 1550 to 1610, more than sixty ships a year sailed between Spain and the Caribbean islands. Spanish sailors crammed the ship's hold, or cargo space, with guns, clothes, glass, paper, and wine to take to the New World. They returned to Spain laden with Caribbean goods such as sugar, tobacco, and spices.

It wasn't long before other nations sent ships to explore. Sailing vessels from England, France, and Holland arrived on Caribbean shores hoping to expand their countries' wealth and increase their territorial holdings.

European colonies flourished in the New World. Two hundred years after Christopher Columbus discovered the Caribbean islands, European settlements had displaced native populations. Colonies of white settlers and their African slaves planted crops and introduced domestic animals such as cattle, goats, hogs, and dogs. Farming and fishing fed the growing population, and sea turtles were an abundant fishery resource.

William Dampier, an English explorer and pirate during the late 1600s, chronicled the skill that native peoples showed in turtle hunting: "They are very ingenious at throwing the Lance, Fisgig, Harpoon, or any manner of Dart. . . . For this they are esteemed and coveted by all Privateers; for one or two of them in a Ship, will maintain 100 Men: So that when we careen our Ships, we choose commonly such Places where there is plenty of Turtle or Manatee for these Moskito men to strike."

European settlers soon learned about the best places to find sea turtles in the Caribbean. Settlements actually grew up around sea turtle nesting areas. While sea turtles spend the vast majority of their time in the ocean, females eventually need to visit a sandy beach, dig a hole, and lay their eggs. During this vulnerable time, females are particularly easy to approach and kill. By the late sixteenth century, turtle meat was in high demand throughout the Caribbean, and experienced hunters routinely traveled to the region's largest nesting colonies. Great fortunes were made in the sea turtle trade, focused mainly on green and hawksbill turtles.

It took five weeks to sail from the Caribbean islands back to England. To keep a hundred-man crew alive on board required plenty of food. Sea turtles proved the perfect ocean-going meat. Sailors flipped the turtles over on their shells and then stacked them below decks on top of each other. Sometimes they reached four or five turtles high. The turtles could live upside down for weeks. Fresh turtle meat during a long ocean trip became all the rage.

Sea turtles were consumed not only in the colonies and on the sailing journeys back home; Europeans craved the meat as well. In particular, green turtle soup became a delicacy throughout Europe, especially in London restaurants. The soup was made from a half-dozen pieces of cartilage known as "calipee." Calipee was cut from the bones of the plastron, or bottom shell.

By the mid-1800s, approximately fifteen thousand turtles a year were being shipped to Europe.

Some biologists estimate that before Columbus arrived in the New World, several hundred million green sea turtles lived in the Caribbean alone. The persecution of turtles for five centuries drastically reduced that wild population. Today, there are about two hundred thousand adult female green turtles throughout the world (estimated from nesting beach studies), a dramatic reduction indeed. Similar historical estimates are not available for leatherbacks because they were not commercially traded and records weren't kept. Although the pressures of hunting sea turtles for food may be a thing of the past, today a whole new army of threats exists to further endanger the remaining sea turtle species.

BEACH CLEANUP

"Here's one, Daddy," says Elijah Liam Segota, chucking a plastic bottle into a large black trash bag held open by his father, James. Elijah's brother, Gabriel, finds one, too.

Elijah and Gabriel are two of the thirty-three people who helped remove 620 pounds of trash from the Keys Beach, a primary nesting spot for leatherback sea turtles on the island of St. Kitts.

For over twenty-five years, the Ocean Conservancy, an organization dedicated to keeping the ocean healthy, has hosted an annual International Coastal Cleanup day. In 2011, more than five hundred thousand volunteers removed over 7.4 million pounds of debris from beaches, lakes, and rivers in 108 countries, including forty-eight states in the United States. The Ocean Conservancy reports that thousands of sea turtles, marine mammals, and seabirds are injured and killed by ocean garbage every year. Loggerhead sea turtles (and many other species as well) get tangled in rope or fishing line, and leatherback turtles gobble plastic bags thinking they are eating their favorite food: jellyfish.

Elijah and Gabriel Segota pick up trash on Keys Beach in St. Kitts. Less trash on the beach makes it easier for sea turtle hatchlings to safely reach the ocean.

MODERN SEA TURTLE THREATS

LONGLINE FISHING

Longline fishing is a commercial fishing technique used throughout the world's seas to catch open-ocean fish such as swordfish, tuna, halibut, and sharks. Fishermen set out a length of mono-filament fishing line from a few miles to sometimes over fifty miles long. Attached to this main line are smaller lines with hooks baited with squid or fish. Often "nontarget" species are hooked, including marine mammals, albatross, and other seabirds, as well as sea turtles, whales, and dolphins. Once caught, the sea turtle is dragged underwater. If the turtle survives to be brought up on deck, it is released only to die later with an ingested three-inch hook (or several hooks) lodged in its throat. According to the U.S. National Marine Fisheries Service, thousands of leatherback and loggerhead sea turtles are killed annually on the longline fishery in the North Atlantic.

A sea turtle with a three-inch fishing hook embedded in its mouth rests on the ocean floor.

GILL NET FISHING

Across the world's oceans and certainly tropical maritime countries where sea turtles congregate to feed or lay eggs, commercial and small-scale fisheries use gill nets. Nets of twine or monofilament are dragged through the water, catching fish by their gills. Sea turtles and other nontarget species are also caught. Turtles tangled in these nets are held underwater and, if the fisherman is not diligently checking his nets often during the day (and night), the turtles will drown. Gill net fishing is one of the oldest fishing techniques in the world. Records of Japanese gill net fishing date back three thousand years. While gill nets are still used in many subsis-

A very serious threat to sea turtles throughout the Caribbean is the entanglement and drowning of sea turtles in fishing nets. Sea turtles are air-breathers, just like you and me, and they drown when held underwater. Uncounted hundreds of thousands of sea turtles are killed in shrimp trawls, long lines, and drift and gill nets every year.

tence fishing communities throughout the world, including the Caribbean Sea, the United Nations banned their use in international waters in 1993 because of the millions upon millions of nontarget species killed every year, many of them classified as endangered species.

Artificial beachfront lighting can disorient the nesting female turtles and also the hatchlings, preventing them from clearly identifying and orienting to the ocean horizon.

HABITAT LOSS

The destruction of nesting beaches can result from erosion, sand mining, seawall construction, and coastal development of houses and hotels. Artificial lighting accompanies much of this construction and can make the area unsuitable for nesting turtles and their young. This is because sea turtles find the sea by using subtle light cues associated with the ocean horizon. Bright lights on the beach confuse the adult females and their newly hatched young, disorienting them inland, away from the sea, and often to their death.

Scientists believe plastic bottles can last for hundreds to thousands of years. Kimberly surveys the plastic pollution washed ashore along a beach in St. Kitts.

MARINE DEBRIS

If you talk to fishermen or others who spend a lot of time on the water, they'll tell you that everything ends up in the ocean. Plastic bags, cigarette butts, plastic toys, Styrofoam packaging, six-pack rings, balloons, aluminum foil, sneakers, bottles, and larger garbage, such as discarded fishing gear, rope, and nets. From ingesting plastic pieces to becoming entangled in old fishing line and nets, turtles face constant hazards as they swim from one foraging ground to another. Scientists estimate that one-third to one-half or more of all sea turtles have ingested deadly plastic debris.

Theophilus Taylor shows Kimberly the gill nets he used to capture sea turtles from his boat.

CHAPTER 3

THE MAN WHO HUNTED SEA TURTLES

Theophilus Taylor

Theophilus Taylor is a sixty-eight-year-old lifelong Kittitian. He is a tall man with a massive smile and hands the size of dinner plates. Throughout his life, Theophilus has used his hands to earn a living. As a young man, he worked long hours under the scorching Caribbean sun in the sugarcane fields. He now tills the earth on his hillside farm, raising fruits and vegetables to sell in the local market. When he is not tending his peanut and cabbage crops, Theophilus (Theo for short) fishes the waters of St. Kitts. He is a well-respected fisherman and is president of the local Sandy Point Fishermen's Cooperative.

A BRIEF HISTORY OF ST. KITTS

Among the first settlers on St. Kitts were the Carib Indians, who named the island Liamuiga, meaning "fertile island." The Caribs occupied St. Kitts for nearly two hundred years. When European sailors discovered the island's abundant rainfall and rich volcanic soils, they set out to make this tropical paradise their own.

From 1493 to 1783, Spanish, French, and British explorers vied for control of the island. While the production of tobacco, cotton, and indigo made many European planters rich, it wasn't until 1640 and the growth of the sugarcane industry that St. Kitts changed forever. With the help of thousands of imported African slaves, whole hillsides were cleared for sugarcane plantations. More than 90 percent of the population of St. Kitts is of African descent.

St. Kitts, along with its smaller neighbor, Nevis, is called a federation; the two-island state is ruled by a prime minister. People from St. Kitts are known as Kittitians, while people on Nevis are called Nevisians.

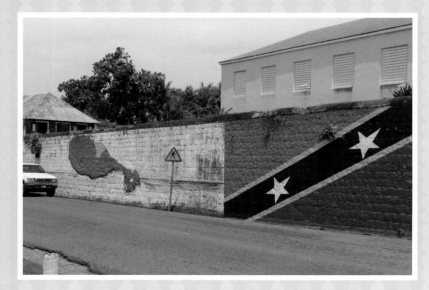

The color green in the St. Kitts flag signifies the island's fertility; red, the struggles of the people, from slavery through colonialism to independence; yellow, year-round sunshine; black, the African heritage of the people; and white stars, hope and liberty, or St. Kitts and Nevis.

Theo was raised by his grandmother and did not grow up eating sea turtle meat. But when he began fishing, sea turtles became part of his catch. One year, he caught fifty-eight sea turtles. For nearly ten years, Theo harvested sea turtles in the waters of St. Kitts. From a thirty-foot wooden boat called *Fubal*, he and his crew of four snagged green and hawksbill sea turtles in large mesh nets. The turtles were hauled ashore, decapitated, and butchered.

News would spread quickly through the village: "Fresh turtle meat!" From large white coolers, townspeople bought the prized turtle flesh. Villagers would pay the local equivalent of two to three U.S. dollars per pound of sea turtle meat.

These days, though, Theo's turtle nets lie tangled and forgotten in a messy clump at the bottom of a wrecked boat. What turned Theo Taylor from a poacher of turtles to a protector of turtles?

The sea turtle slaughterer met the sea turtle scientist in 2006.

"The fishermen butchered the turtles right beside the road," says Kimberly. "While it was pretty hard to watch, having access to so many turtle carcasses allowed us to gather a tremendous amount of data, making each animal as valuable as possible. We would perform a full physical exam, including taking blood samples before the turtles were killed.

"We used the blood samples to establish baseline parameters for these animals. Later, in the laboratory, we'd look at nutritional status, contaminants, and so forth. After the animal's death, we would perform a full necropsy, taking tissue samples. We recovered all stomach contents and then analyzed them to determine what the turtles had been eating.

"We'd sometimes see flipper-tagged animals," continues Kimberly. "The tags would provide lots of information about where the animal was originally tagged, migratory patterns, growth size, and so on. We once saw a hawksbill turtle tagged from Nicaragua. It was the longest distance for a tag return we ever found.

"I always made sure that I removed the sea turtle carapace," says Kimberly, "so that turtle shells did not end up in the marketplace for sale." Nearly all nations of the world prohibit international trade in sea turtle products, so purchasing an item made from sea turtle shell can land someone in a lot of trouble.

The fishermen were always very good about letting Kimberly and the other turtle researchers know when they were butchering sea turtles. At about the same time that Kimberly began to work the sea turtle harvest, she started a series of sea turtle talks for the local St. Kitts fishermen. "It was a little like walking into enemy territory," she says. "One fisherman walked out after five minutes."

Gradually, the scientist and many of the St. Kitts fishermen developed mutual trust.

"The fishermen are amazing surgeons," says Kimberly. "With a five-inch knife, they can carve and trim and surgically remove nearly all the flesh from a sea turtle. Their knowledge of the animal's internal organs is impressive."

Kimberly witnessed more turtle harvesting than she wishes to remember. But, over time, she forged a working relationship with Theo, one of the leading fishermen in Sandy Point. After more than four years of working side by side with Theo on turtle harvesting, scientist and fisherman established a strong bond. One day, Kimberly, along with the Georgia Sea Turtle Center, broached the topic of conservation. "We discussed the fact," Kimberly says, "that if we did not work more on conservation, sea turtles would not be around for his grandchildren and great-grandchildren to see. I asked if Theo would like to begin leading a sea turtle satellite tracking project in St. Kitts. Theo became an eager amateur scientist."

Kimberly eventually got Theo to join her team on a turtle patrol.

In St. Kitts, sea turtle meat serves as a source of both protein and income. "Harvesting sea turtles was definitely a money-making practice for Theo and his crew," says Kimberly. "Over time, several options to the sea turtle harvest were put into practice in

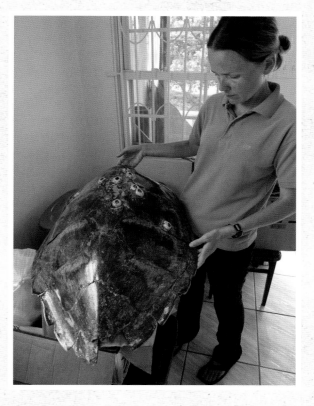

Kimberly with a confiscated hawksbill sea turtle shell. Under a conservation treaty between countries called CITES (Convention on International Trade in Endangered Species), the trading of sea turtle shells and other products is illegal. Most sea turtle laws, however, include a minimum size limit, which focuses the harvest on breeding adults and has been disastrous for Caribbean populations, including St. Kitts.

St. Kitts, including sea turtle ecotourism, research technician positions, and the Beach Bottle Bead program. This program was developed by WIDECAST and is now offered Caribbean-wide. In this program, islanders are trained to make jewelry from shards of broken beer and liquor bottles collected from nesting beaches and from litter in local communities. Tumbled smooth by the ocean, or transformed by flame into glass beads, the recycled glass contributes to local economies through the sale of finished pieces to tourists.

"With a little design work," says Kimberly, "the natural sea glass, as well as our flame-worked beads, can be turned into stunning pendants, earrings, key chains, and more! The colors are fantastic. Sky blue. Rainforest green. Pale red. Tourists are drawn to island-made jewelry, and we soon realized that broken and discarded glass could be a source of income to help pay the sea turtle fishermen.

"I don't think jewelry alone will end the turtle harvest, but a combination of alternative livelihoods will. These include ecotourism—guided tours providing an opportunity to watch the nesting process or participate in morning patrols, nest excavations, and so on—craft making, and small business endeavors such as a gift shop. The interpretive center will bring all of this together. There will be an area for educational displays (visitors will pay a nominal entrance fee), an area for craft making where visitors can view and participate in the process and also make purchases, a marine conservation–themed gift shop, a sea turtle hospital and rehabilitation area, a turtle watch orientation area, school field trips, and so on. The center will serve as a central base to ensure that sea turtle research and conservation in St. Kitts are community-centered and financially self-sustainable."

Despite all of these efforts, people still eat sea

Theo and Kimberly investigate a leatherback nesting track.

turtle meat legally in St. Kitts. "An open harvest on sea turtles still exists every year from October 1 to February 28 in St. Kitts," says Kimberly. "That means fishermen can capture and kill as many sea turtles as they can catch, as long as each exceeds a minimum weight." Kimberly will know that she is successful when three things happen: St. Kitts declares a moratorium on killing sea turtles; former turtle fishermen are meaningfully engaged in other income-earning endeavors; and her dream of a St. Kitts biodiversity site on Keys Beach with a state-of-the-art sustainable nature center is realized.

As for Theophilus Taylor, he harvested his last sea turtle in the fall of 2009.

"Oh, no, mon," says Theo, dragging up a clump of unused turtle net. "No more sea turtle killing for me. It was the turtle lady who changed me." He is now an enthusiastic and learned member of Kimberly's St. Kitts Sea Turtle Monitoring Network (SKSTMN).

"I have been working with Theophilus since 2006," says Kimberly. "In the years between 2006 and 2010, when he would capture or slaughter a turtle, I was called to collect biological information on the animal. In October 2010, Theo agreed to work with me placing transmitters on sea turtles and then going into the school system to educate children about sea turtles and the ocean journeys that the transmitters would document. For the first school presentation, he chose to visit

Theo shows off his peanut harvest at his farm under the shadow of Mount Liamuiga.

Newton Ground Primary, the school he attended as a child. I remember that as he called the assembly of around two hundred children to order he said, 'Did you know a sea turtle can carry a message around the world on its back?' This was the moment I knew he was invested in the project and conservation."

These days, during peak sea turtle nesting from April to July, Theo is on a rotating five-nights-a-week turtle patrol. From September

During Sea Turtle Camp, Theo gets dressed as a leatherback sea turtle to the delight of all the campers.

through the end of February he conducts morning patrols on many St. Kitts beaches. He records hawksbill and green sea turtle nests and follows them until hatching. During the off-season, Kimberly and Theo visit the island's thirty schools, giving presentations on sea turtles.

Sea turtles could not have two more enthusiastic advocates.

HOW GLASS SAVES SEA TURTLES

Kimberly was attending the WIDECAST Annual Meeting in 2006 when Dr. Karen Eckert, the executive director, talked about JoBean Chambers, a professional glass artist living in the Dutch Caribbean island of Saba. Karen had been an invited speaker at Saba's annual Sea & Learn conference and had spent time in Jo's studio, learning to make beads. As they talked, it became clear that the same techniques Jo was teaching her art students could be used in making recycled glass beads to generate income for communities working in sea turtle conservation.

"At our annual meeting, Karen shared this story with us, and showed examples of the beads she had made in Jo's workshop," Kimberly says. "Later, in 2009, a Global Environmental Facility Small Grants Program provided the funds we needed to bring the Beach Bottle Bead program to St. Kitts as a potential alternative source of income for sea turtle fishermen. Jo was invited to St. Kitts to train interested persons, and she returned several times to help us. Soon the sea turtle group here had established a glass arts shop and was producing a variety of lovely items."

WIDECAST has also facilitated trainings in Trinidad, St. Vincent, and Antigua. "The recycled beads are unique and tourists love them!" says Kimberly. "Here in St. Kitts we had a few logistical obstacles to overcome, like the price of pure compressed oxygen, which is really expensive here. The challenge was solved with the purchase of an oxygen generator. We also decided to incorporate the natural sea glass whenever we can because it lends a special island charm to the crafter's work. We love being involved in the WIDECAST network, because it's so solution oriented!"

Members of the St. Kitts community volunteer to make jewelry at the Beach Bottle Bead Shop, an alternative livelihood program designed in partnership with WIDECAST.

Kimberly picks up handfuls of broken beach glass along the darkly flecked sandy beaches of St. Kitts. Red glass is the most prized.

Kimberly sweeps the remains of the leatherback nest into the sandy cavity, thereby providing nutrients that contribute to the survival of other beach creatures.

CHAPTER 4

SCIENCE IS HANDS-AND-KNEES WORK

O n a dazzling morning in late May, Dr. Kimberly Stewart marches along Keys Beach, on the northern end of St. Kitts. It is just past nine and the Caribbean sun already scorches the black-flecked sand. Kimberly is sporting her usual beach footwear: flip-flops. Her toenails are painted blue, her favorite color.

Two stragglers from the unearthed nest take a tentative crawl near the surf line under the watchful eyes of Kimberly.

What is on the agenda this morning? Nest excavation.

Leatherbacks begin nesting in St. Kitts in March annually. Approximately sixty to sixty-five days after the mother leatherback completes her nest and returns to the sea, the eggs begin to hatch. The long period during which turtles return again and again to lay eggs allows Kimberly to watch adult turtles nest and the young hatch during the same window of time. Two to three days after the hatchlings leave a nest, Kimberly and her crew of turtle watchers return to dig it up and have a look.

"We try to perform an excavation on each nest," says Kimberly. "In a perfect world we would. The only reason we do not get to all of them is a shortage of staff."

Turtle scientists keep meticulous records. Kimberly knows which nests have hatched as well as which nests are about to hatch. Good science also means careful observation. Because much of the life history of the leatherback turtle, in particular, is still such a mystery, scientists take every opportunity to study what they can, when they can. Investigating a leatherback nest is like uncovering hidden treasure. Even after the mother leatherback has returned to sea, the nest she leaves behind provides scientists with a wealth of information.

"We perform an excavation so that we can determine hatch success in the nest," says Kimberly. "Also, in some cases we can look at the contents of an unhatched (or incompletely hatched) nest and speculate on what may have gone wrong. It is important to know how many females you have nesting and how many eggs were laid, but without the hatch data, you don't really know how many young you may be putting back into the ocean."

Nest excavation is hands-and-knees work. Kimberly kneels beside the wooden stake, marking the site of the leatherback nest, and begins to scoop out the first few fistfuls of sand. Her records tell her that the hatchlings left this nest two nights ago.

As the hole gets deeper and deeper, hands and knees turn into full body contact with the beach. Kimberly lies face down on the sand and excavates one handful at a time. Reaching down into the turtle hole, her fingers finally locate an eggshell. One by one, Kimberly hauls up the remains of the old nest into the light of day.

"We count three things during a nest

Sea turtle researchers use wooden stakes to mark where nests are located. Two or three days after the hatchlings emerge, researchers return to dig up the nest and have a look.

Kimberly pulls leatherback eggs into the light of day to see what they will tell her about how productive the nest was.

Kimberly counts and records the eggs that hatched, the unhatched eggs, and the yolk-less eggs.

Leatherback nests often have one or two hatchlings who break out after the main group has left. These late hatchers are called stragglers.

excavation," says Kimberly, her cheek resting on the face of the dune as she probes the sand with her fingertips, finding the eggs by feel. "The unhatched eggs, the hatched ones, and the yolkless eggs. By digging up the nest, we get a good glimpse at the productivity."

Kimberly checks out the contents of an un-hatched egg. "We are increasingly concerned about global climate change and its effects on nest temperatures," she says. "This is a nest with more unhatched eggs than hatched ones. Are we looking at a crisis?"

Kimberly gently removes a sand-spattered leatherback hatchling. "Oh, look what we have here!" she says. She flips open the top of a small red cooler, places the baby turtle into the shaded confines, and shuts the lid. "With leatherbacks it has been pretty common to

find one or two stragglers left behind in the bottom of the nest, still trying to get out."

As she finishes her sentence, she recovers another small turtle. This one joins its nest mate in the cooler.

"Hatchlings work as a group to dig their way to the surface," says Kimberly. "If there are any late hatchers in the nest that emerge from the egg after the main group has already left, then they generally cannot make it out on their own. It is much harder for one or two turtles to reach the surface of the beach. In addition to late hatchers, some of the hatch-lings may just be weaker or have slight de-formities that prevent them from keeping up with the group, and they can be left behind."

Once she has removed all the unhatched eggs and shells and carefully organized them beside the nest cavity, it's time to record the data. Kimberly squats on the beach, her legs, arms, and latex-shielded hands plastered with sand. "I eat, sleep, breathe sand. It's in my hair. It's in my car. It's in my house. It's all part of the job," she says. She grabs a stiff white card called the St. Kitts Sea Turtle Monitoring Network Data Sheet, which is similar to the data sheet used by other mem-bers of the professional WIDECAST net-work, and goes to work filling out the details. She records that this nest had twenty-one unhatched eggs, fifteen hatched eggs, and twenty-two yolkless eggs.

After recording the nest information on the data sheet, Kimberly sweeps the entire batch of broken and examined turtle eggs back into the hole. She covers the debris with sand and tamps it down. The turtle egg remains will provide nutrients for beach crabs, ants, bacteria, and many other organisms along the beach. Plant roots also benefit from the decomposing turtle eggs by absorbing needed minerals and organic matter.

As she works, Kimberly wonders out loud how many males and how many females were in the nest that she had dug. "The sex of a sea turtle hatchling is not determined at the moment of fertilization but during the incubation process," she says, striding down the beach to another excavation. "Whether the hatchling is male or female is determined by the temperature in the nest."

It's called TSD, or temperature-dependent sex determination. Scientists have discovered that warmer nest temperatures favor the production of females, while cooler nest temperatures favor the production of males. "Hot chicks, cool dudes," says Kimberly. "It's an easy way to remember it." While there are no definitive answers as to why this happens, many scientists believe that it was caused by evolutionary pressures millions of years ago.

"Global climate change has scientists increasingly concerned," continues Kimberly on a more somber note. "Populations of species with temperature-dependent sex determination may serve as ideal indicators of the biological impact of global temperature change."

One scientific study on the painted turtle revealed that even a slight increase in summer heat could alter the nest temperature, thereby skewing the ratio of females and males. Scientific models predict a rise of as much as 39 degrees Fahrenheit (°F), or 4 degrees Celsius (°C), in July temperatures for North America within the next hundred years. If this were to occur it could result in the extinction of the painted turtle population because no males would be produced from nests in the warmer soils. Already scientists have shown that loggerhead sea turtles in Florida are nesting later each year, a shift attributed to climate change.

"My main concerns," says Kimberly, "aside from the obvious threat of coastal erosion and beach loss associated with sea level rise, would be feminization and embryo mortality as temperatures increase. Temperatures above 90°F (32°C) can be lethal to embryos." For a species that's already in danger, this isn't good news.

A leatherback hatchling marches forward to the sea, over sticks, around clumps of seaweed, up and down tracks in the sand.

CHAPTER 5

THE JOURNEY OF THE HATCHLINGS

Alligator and crocodile moms make the best parents in the reptile world. They will guard a nest once the babies are born, actually helping their young out of their eggs. Sea turtles, on the other hand, are barely present when it comes to parental care. The father leatherback, after mating, vanishes. The mother offers what care she can, but of necessity that care is limited to protecting her developing embryos by encasing them in

Female sea turtles generally lay 80 to 100 or more leathery-shelled white eggs. The exact number of eggs may vary from 50 to 250, depending on the species. Most females nest two to five times per year, again depending on the species.

a soft shell drawn from the precious calcium in her own bones, carefully selecting a nest site safe from the dangerous waves of the sea, burying her eggs deep in the sand, and camouflaging them to hide them from hungry predators.

A clutch of turtle eggs left in the sand is a package of protein that few predators can ignore. The turtle nest is most at risk during egg laying and hatching. Dogs and wild hogs can come up behind an egg-laying female sea turtle and devour her eggs on the spot. Other predators, such as vultures, mongoose, rats, raccoons, cats, crabs, and, of course, people, will also consume turtle eggs. If the turtle nest escapes detection from predators, the young may be safe until it is time to leave the nest.

The hatchlings have a caruncle (egg tooth) at the tip of their beak. This sharp, bony tip will help them slice through the eggshell. The caruncle is temporary and disappears a short time after hatching. Once the hatchling has ripped a hole in the shell, the amniotic fluids that surrounded the baby turtle drain away.

A bucket of leatherback eggs. The leathery eggs are two inches wide, about the size of a cue ball.

How does a three-and-a-half-inch leatherback hatchling break free of its shell and dig through more than two feet of hard-packed sand to the surface? With a little help from its friends.

Leaving a sea turtle nest is a group effort. Hatchlings work as a team to get to the top of the sand. Scientists call this a display of mutualism, or teamwork that is vital to survival.

How did scientists figure out that hatchlings work together to leave a nest? They dug a large viewing area and placed a pane of glass on one side of the sea turtle clutch and watched how the hatchlings made it to the surface. As one hatchling wriggles free of its shell, this action triggers movement in its neighbors. As more and more hatchlings break free of their shells, a sort of frenzied digging occurs. Hatchlings instinctively know which direction is up. The hatchlings at the top layer of the nest scrape and dig at the ceiling of sand above them. As the ceiling of sand collapses, the hatchlings below push and flick the falling sand beneath them. The hatchlings on the sides scratch at the walls. All this digging acts to collapse the sand above, and the hatchlings rise up like an elevator of sea turtles.

This elevator to the surface of the beach makes plenty of stops. The baby turtles rest along the way. After each extended calm, which allows needed oxygen to seep back into the nest cavity, one turtle will start to flail, setting the whole group to flailing, and up they go again. The trip from bottom to top involves a lot of stop and go and takes several days.

Once the hatchling group arrives near the surface, about two or three inches from breaking through, if they sense the time is right, they emerge at once. Sometimes the hatchlings stop and wait, as if pausing to reconsider. They are actually gauging whether the temperature is suitable. Think about it. If you're a baby sea turtle, when is the best time to emerge? Break out during the heat of the day and the little turtles would fry on the hot sand. Plus a daytime journey to the ocean is fraught with dangers because more predators are on the prowl. When the sand cools, the hatchlings sense that the sun is setting and it is time to go. Early evening and all through the night, the hatchlings erupt from the sand and the mad dash to the sea is on.

As the hatchlings boil up from the nest and onto the surface of the beach, they open their eyes for the first time. Almost instantly, the first hatchlings to emerge begin to orient themselves toward the sea. For many years, scientists never understood how turtle hatchlings made their way unerringly down the ocean. Now this rush to the sea is no longer a mystery.

The hatchlings find the water by seeing that the light above the ocean is brighter than the relative darkness of the dunes and vegetation, so they make their way toward the light. Scientists call this a visual cue.

"It's pretty cool to watch the sea-finding ability of baby turtles," says Kimberly. "They pile out of their nest and within seconds it seems they have engaged their GPS. There's

Leatherback hatchlings push up from their underground nest cavity and within seconds are dashing toward the ocean.

not a lot of milling around as hatchlings ask, 'Which way do we go?' As a group, they know exactly where they're going. And they waste no time getting there."

But the path to the ocean is not always an easy one.

A three-and-a-half-inch hatchling scrambling to the sea might have to circumnavigate a log or a plastic bottle. To a hatchling, a tire track can be as wide as a canyon. But watch baby turtles race to the sea and you realize they've got what it takes. Over millions of years, hatchlings have evolved with an overwhelming single-mindedness once they emerge from the nest — to get to the sea in the fastest and most direct way. If they bump into a branch or clump of seaweed, they just go around it, and then continue their beeline to the water. They are determined to reach their destination. It takes a sea turtle hatchling two to three minutes to get from nest cavity to the sea. Those few minutes are filled with hazards. It could get caught by a ghost crab or snatched by a yellow-crowned night heron or picked off by a mongoose or vulture or wild cat or dog or any other hatchling-eating predator. A defenseless, soft-shelled sea turtle makes a tasty treat.

Besides predators, the other major threat to hatchlings is artificial light on the beach or along the coast. Hatchling eyes are extremely sensitive to light. They use this ability to see subtle differences in light, and they use these differences to guide them to the ocean. Lights on a nesting beach from hotels, shops, street lamps, or tennis courts can disorient and confuse hatchlings. Scientists call this light pollution.

"The best beach would be a beach with

A ghost crab uses its front pincers to grab a hatchling on its march to the sea.

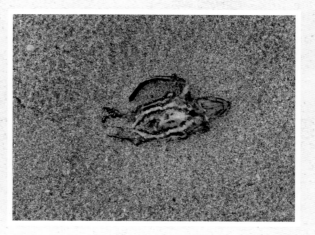

A leatherback hatchling stopped dead in its tracks.

intact vegetation and dunes and no artificial lighting. The vegetation and dune shadows would help hatchlings orient away from this darker background and toward the open ocean's horizon," says Kimberly. "On St. Kitts, the lights from the village in Keys disorient hatchlings on Keys Beach, and they head in the opposite direction in areas where there is no vegetation blocking these lights from them. They are drawn to the brighter lights and end up on the soccer field. On some beaches in St. Kitts the light pollution has been so intense that hatchlings have been disoriented and ended up in the road and eventually crushed by traffic."

If sea turtle hatchlings can survive the biggest dash of their lives and make it to the sea, their marine life begins. Of the hatchlings born on St. Kitts, only females will

return — decades in the future — when it is time to crawl up this beach or one nearby to nest. If the hatchling is a male, he will never set flipper on land again, unless it washes up sick, injured, or dead.

Left: A leatherback hatchling scuttles to the sea. If the hatchling becomes hopelessly tangled in a length of monofilament fishing line it becomes easy prey for ghost crabs, dogs, mongooses, or night herons.

A street lamp draws a leatherback hatchling away from the ocean and towards possible death.

Once in the water, hatchlings use incoming waves to orient themselves to the open sea. They fly through the water, using their front flippers to propel them and their rear flippers to steer. Hatchlings often take shelter in floating mats of seaweed and other oceanic accumulations that provide food and refuge during the first few years of life.

CHAPTER 6

THE MYSTERY OF HATCHLING TURTLES

Where does a little leatherback sea turtle go when it disappears into the waves? Scientists don't have a clue!

From left to right, hawksbill, green, and leatherback sea turtle hatchlings reveal a lighter shade on their plastrons, so to predatory fish below them they blend in with the brightness at the surface.

"One thing we do know," says Kimberly, watching over two nest stragglers near the ocean's edge, "predation doesn't end once the hatchlings reach the water. The attacks come from above and below. Frigate birds, gulls, and other seabirds pluck hatchlings from the water. Sharks, barracuda, tarpon, jack, snapper, and other predatory fish take a lot of the hatchlings entering the ocean."

In Australia, scientists have determined that the greatest predation occurs when green sea turtle hatchlings cross the Great Barrier Reef, heading to the open ocean. In one study, predatory fish consumed as many as 85 percent of hatchlings within the first hour after they entered the sea. Healthy coral reefs abound with fish, and sea turtle hatchlings must traverse these dangerous waters in

A hawksbill hatchling rests in a mat of Sargassum weed, which provides sea turtle hatchlings with shelter from predators and a place to rest and find food.

When a hatchling reaches deep water, it enters a driftline of seaweed and other algae where it finds food and shelter. These areas might be considered moving, open-sea nursery grounds. Some seaweed mats, like the central Atlantic's Sargasso Sea, are enormous, forcing the largest of ships to navigate around them. The early phases of a sea turtle's life are often called the "lost years," because the precise pathways taken before it grows to the size of a dinner plate and returns to coastal waters are unknown.

As with so many things pertaining to sea turtles, the leatherback turtle is an exception to the rule. Being the most pelagic, or adapted to the open ocean, of the marine turtles, it is thought that leatherback hatchlings, when they reach the water, make straight for the high seas and stay there, forgoing the relative safety of the seaweed mats and driftlines.

Dr. Scott Eckert of WIDECAST says, "Despite a growing understanding of the developmental life stages and habitats utilized by the young of most sea turtle species, there is no information on where hatchling leatherback turtles go after leaving the nesting beaches."

A decade ago, Scott put on his Sherlock Holmes hat and decided to piece together all

order to reach their oceanic nursery grounds. Females lay thousands of eggs over the course of their adult lives to compensate for this and many other sources of mortality.

For some turtle species, including leatherbacks, evolution provides hatchlings a little help against predators by supplying them with what scientists refer to as "counter-shading." They are dark on the top and light on the bottom. To predatory seabirds, the darkish carapace of the hatchling blends in with the dark ocean waters, and to predatory fish below, the light underside blends in with the bright light coming from the surface.

Baby hatchlings swim at right angles to the waves (an action called "wave compass"), which helps them reach deep offshore waters as soon as possible.

The headlong charge of hatchlings out to deep water is known as a "swim frenzy." Hatchlings are good swimmers from day one. Many turtles, including leatherbacks, have small ridges along their backs that allow them to swim more quickly and efficiently through the water. They also have enough leftover egg yolk in their bellies to last several days, so they do not need to stop to feed in predator-rich coastal waters.

IN-WATER TAGGING AND LAB WORK

To get a more thorough view of what's happening with the sea turtle population around St. Kitts, the St. Kitts Sea Turtle Monitoring Network In-Water Team conducts surveys of foraging sea turtle populations in St. Kitts. "We don't capture adults or subadults during In-Water," says Kimberly. "They are too large, and we are working the near-shore bays."

Leatherbacks remain elusively offshore in deep water between nestings, and return to high-seas feeding grounds when the egg-laying season is complete. But other sea turtle species live in the coastal waters of St. Kitts year-round; their brief capture, study, and release provide information critical to their protection and can help define actions necessary to safeguard their preferred habitats.

"One of the other issues with catching sea turtles," says Kimberly, "is breath control. Sea turtles can hold their breath for several hours when they are at rest, whereas humans can barely manage a minute or so. Because our speed and breath-holding abilities are no match for sea turtles, our opportunities for capture usually come when the turtle is resting on the bottom or slowly

A volunteer captures a live green sea turtle.

gliding over the reef. In that case, we can often approach from behind, while other members of our team distract the turtle from the front. Also, when the animal is coming up for breath, it is a bit easier to catch it as it moves to the surface."

Once the turtles are captured, they are weighed, measured, photographed, and tagged, at minimum. If the turtle relieves itself, Kimberly looks for parasites. Over time, these data help scientists understand growth rates, food preferences, habitat use, changing ratios of males to females and young turtles to older turtles, and so on. Studies

"We like to have the turtles out no more than fifteen minutes," says Kimberly. "If we are applying tags, extracting blood, taking measurements, etc., and the animal is overheating, we will douse the turtle with a gallon of seawater."

Kimberly holds a young green turtle while a volunteer attaches a metal tag to the rear of the turtle's flipper.

led by veterinarians like Kimberly involve blood and tissue sampling that are used to define the genetic makeup and health status of a population.

An evening or night emergence serves the hatchlings well because most predators are not active at night. In addition, the sand is relatively cool and the bright ocean horizon is a strong orientation clue. Contrary to popular belief, hatchlings do not orient toward the moon. Their eyes are very sensitive to light, and under natural conditions the open ocean horizon is always brighter than the darker landward vegetation. For this reason, artificial beachfront lighting is a serious threat to the newborns — it confuses them and can direct them away from the sea.

the records of young leatherback sightings. He focused his data collection on the size of the juvenile, where it was found, and the temperature of the water.

Female leatherbacks usually take one to two hours to crawl out of the ocean, dig a body pit, make a nest cavity, lay eggs, cover them up, camouflage the nest site, and return to the ocean.

"I was very careful to evaluate each report for accuracy," says Scott. "If there was any question as to location accuracy, size of turtle, or other such information, the record was rejected from my analysis. One hundred records of juvenile leatherbacks qualified for my analysis."

He found an intriguing pattern. Leatherbacks with a curved carapace length of less than 3.2 feet (about 100 centimeters) were found only in water temperature above 79°F (26°C). Leatherbacks with a slightly larger shell of 3.5 feet (107 centimeters) or more were found in waters as cold as 54°F (12°C). In other words, small leatherbacks stay in warm waters, while larger leatherbacks can live in cooler oceans. Interestingly, scientists cannot yet relate the size of a leatherback to

its age. Juveniles are so rarely seen that their growth rates have not been documented in the wild.

"The relationship between the distribution of small leatherbacks and temperature is an important clue to understanding the life history of this unique species," says Scott. "Leatherbacks appear to spend the first portion of their lives — on average, between twelve and fourteen years — in tropical waters. Once they exceed a hundred centimeters in carapace length, however, they can move into the cooler waters that have long been considered the primary habitat for the species."

Because mother turtles pass a genetic signature to their daughters, and daughters return, as egg-bearing adults, to the beaches where they were born, the sea turtles using a particular nesting beach have a genetic "fingerprint" that allows scientists to match young turtles feeding in the waters of one country to their nesting beaches of origin, which can be thousands of miles away. "Advanced techniques such as these encourage countries to work together to protect shared sea turtle populations," says Dr. Karen Eckert.

Sea turtles have an amazing fidelity to the beach or coastal area where they were born. Scientists call this "natal beach homing" — a kind of sea turtle global positioning system.

When sea turtles enter the ocean as hatch-

A leatherback begins a long dive to perhaps four thousand feet! Leatherbacks have the ability to store high amounts of oxygen within their blood and muscle tissues. This allows them to dive deep in search of prey and hold their breath underwater for up to seventy minutes.

lings, they might swim for fifteen to thirty years before returning to their home beach. Think about that! An animal that can pinpoint the exact beach on which it was hatched even after spending decades on the open seas and possibly from thousands of miles away on the other side of an ocean basin. How does it accomplish these incredible feats?

Despite decades of study, scientists are still searching for answers concerning sea turtle navigation. The development of tracking devices and advances in microtechnology, and some creative laboratory-based experimentation, have helped researchers learn more about

the secrets behind long-distance travels of sea turtles. The current understanding is that sea turtles use a number of tools to help them navigate through the world's oceans. They may be able to migrate across an ocean basin using a magnetic map that they have stored in their memory. It also appears that sea turtles can use visual cues, and possibly remember chemical signatures from specific coastal regions. Some scientists speculate that sea turtles may orient by hearing low-frequency sounds of the coastline up to hundreds of kilometers away. Although scientists are slowly unraveling some of the mysteries of sea turtle

navigation, there are many puzzles yet to be solved. Scientists still know almost nothing about male sea turtles, who spend their whole lives at sea. "We've never sighted an adult male with our In-Water Team," says Kimberly. "Mating likely takes place far from shore, away from curious scientific eyes."

TRACKING SEA TURTLES

We seem to know so much about leatherbacks—and yet so little. Where do they go? What do they do? How do they do it? And why are they disappearing from the planet?

One reason, says Dr. Scott Eckert of WIDECAST, is that "leatherbacks are very hard to track. One of the concerns we had from the start was the delicate skin. It is actually less leatherlike, but more rubbery, paper thin and very fragile, almost like a high-speed swimmer's suit. You couldn't attach a tracking device to their shells with glue or screws," he says. So he had to develop a special harness to carry tracking instruments.

Like a lot of scientists, Scott is a fan of hybridizing research fields. He worked with marine mammal scientist Gerry Kooyman, who developed a device called a time-depth recorder (TDR) for emperor penguins and seals in Antarctica. "The great thing about scientists sharing their studies is that I could teach Gerry about sea turtles and he could teach me stuff about marine mammals and penguins."

One of the first things Scott learned

Dr. Scott Eckert with a leatherback.

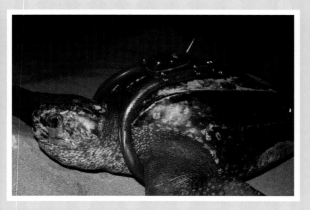

This leatherback is fitted with a VHF transmitter that allows scientists to monitor its short-range movements.

when he put TDRs on leatherbacks was that they're incredible divers—they dive to more than four thousand feet!

Why would an animal dive that deep? Were they feeding? In all good science, you develop a theory, or hypothesis, and then you go out and test it. Scott attached more instruments, including VHF radio transmitters, to a harness on the leatherbacks to monitor their movements in the ocean, and ultramarine velocity recorders to measure how far and how fast they swim.

"When a turtle returned to the beach to lay her next clutch of eggs, we were able to recover the instruments, download the data to our computers, analyze the information, and puzzle over the distinct day and night dive pattern.

Leatherbacks are exclusive jellyfish eaters, and it turns out that they were following the jellyfish as they retreated to the ocean depths during the day, and then the turtles followed the jellies up near the surface at night."

Kimberly attaches PIT tags to the leatherbacks on St. Kitts. How are they part of the data-collecting process?

"A PIT tag uniquely identifies the animal so that you can count it within the population, document its nesting and movement patterns, and know that others can identify it, too. The remote technologies that we attached to our leatherbacks—VHF radio transmitters, satellite transmitters, and various types of data loggers (heart rate, swim speed, dive duration and depth)—are designed to provide other data."

Starting in the early 1990s, Scott began to attach satellite transmitters to the leatherback's harness. "I can now track leatherbacks in the Pacific Ocean and in the Atlantic Ocean, all using the same tracking technique, simultaneously from my laptop. It's a great way for scientists to get out to sea—and see what's happening without getting their feet wet. And what we're learning is phenomenal! Leatherbacks are averaging ten thousand kilometers a year! These are similar to the travels of the great whales, like blue whales and humpbacks."

Why do leatherbacks travel such great distances across the world's oceans? To fulfill two very simple needs: to feed and to breed.

Scott explains that despite having a brain the size of your thumb, leatherbacks are incredible navigators. So while they are not the great thinkers of the animal kingdom, they operate on instinct and are seamlessly programmed. The leatherbacks feed on jellyfish for a few months. At some point, perhaps as the jellyfish numbers begin to taper off, the leatherbacks leave these waters and swim to the coast of Africa. Why

make that three-thousand-mile journey? Because they know that by the time they get there, coastal monsoons will provide the right conditions for a very productive jellyfish population. And they feed there for a few months.

"Here's an animal that can actually anticipate a food source thousands of miles away and many months into the future," Scott says. "How do they do it? We don't know."

But all the accumulated scientific knowledge can help save this endangered species.

"You've got to know the whole picture and respond to threats as quickly as possible," says Scott. "The prognosis for the leatherback sea turtle on the planet is mixed. While the Pacific population looks very grim, the Atlantic population shows encouraging signs of stability, even increase. If we work together—all of us—stay vigilant, and scramble to save what's there, we may have leatherbacks swimming in our seas for future generations."

The Chrysaora jellyfish, or stinging sea nettle, is found in abundance from the waters of southern New England to as far south as the coast of Brazil. Leatherbacks eat Chrysaora and are not bothered by the jellyfish's stinging toxins.

Kimberly photographs a leatherback turtle after a very early morning nesting on Keys Beach.

44

CHAPTER 7

It Takes a Community to Save a Sea Turtle

I t takes a community to save a sea turtle," says Kimberly, borrowing a phrase. "We do lots and lots of outreach. For example, using WIDECAST's Sun, Sand & Sea Turtles curriculum, we started an annual Sea Turtle Camp in 2007, and to date we've taught around five hundred children in St. Kitts. If you graduate from Sea Turtle Camp, you are considered a Junior Conservationist with the St. Kitts Sea Turtle Monitoring Network. You and your parents can join our nightly patrol team during the next nesting season."

Jane Sandquist, superintendent of the Ross University Preparatory School, and all the school's students are big supporters of sea turtles and Kimberly's efforts to save sea turtles on St. Kitts.

Kimberly also has a large e-mail listserv and sends out calls for volunteers through it. SKSTMN has an active Facebook page, maintains a website, and does regular radio and television interviews to talk about sea turtle conservation.

The program runs the Sea Turtle Hotline twenty-four hours a day, seven days a week, taking any sea turtle–related questions, as well

Sea Turtle Camp kids check out a young tortoise.

as requests for volunteer positions. If you count ecotourists, sea turtle campers, and beach cleanup folks, more than six hundred people directly participate in the conservation work on St. Kitts every year, most of them as volunteers.

"I love the challenge of managing all of these activities," Kimberly says. "I set out to be a veterinarian. Who would have guessed I would be developing a sea turtle–related microenterprise, working with fishermen, teaching Sea Turtle Camp, and mentoring young conservationists? I love every aspect of it."

Another key way Kimberly reaches out to the community is by participating in fairs and festivals. At St. Kitts country fairs and local science fairs, she sets up educational booths and displays, talks to visitors about sea turtle research and conservation issues, and hands out brochures. Stanley Knight and his family stopped by the St. Kitts Sea Turtle Monitoring Network's education booth at an agricultural fair. "They had lived all their lives on the island and had never seen a nesting sea turtle. Later they contacted us through our Sea Turtle Hotline number and learned about the turtle patrol," says Kimberly.

During the height of the leatherback-nesting season, the last week in May, Stanley and his wife, Tessa, and daughters, fourth-grader Zidane and eighth-grader Kimi-Lee, joined Kimberly on North Friars Beach. Night after night during the turtle season, researchers pack

up their gear and arrive on beaches like this to begin their nightly patrols. While the hours are long and the work, at times, repetitious, every piece of data collected contributes to the big picture, and to the overall goal of better understanding how sea turtles can be saved.

North Friars Beach, a beautiful and wide arc of sand about a mile long, lies on a relatively undeveloped peninsula of St. Kitts. Tourists don't come here because the road in is unmarked. There are no amenities. Residents avoid the place because the surf is treacherous. In other words, it's perfect for nesting sea turtles.

"Some nights we get three or four females coming up to nest and there's plenty of action," says Kimberly. "Some nights not a single turtle, and the minutes stretch into hours."

Suddenly, about two hundred feet ahead, they spot a dark blob in the sand, and freeze.

"Stay put," whispers Kimberly. "I'll check it out."

Everyone waits with bated breath as the turtle scientist creeps up behind the dark shape in the sand. Within moments, Kimberly returns.

"It's a leatherback!" says Kimberly. "She's digging the nest cavity. But I'm concerned that she is too close to the high-tide line. We'll wait a few minutes and move in for a closer look."

Of all the sea turtles, leatherbacks have the habit of nesting closest to the sea. Scientists are

A sign at the parking lot of North Friars Beach warns visitors away from swimming.

A female leatherback rests her head in the sand dune as she focuses on digging a nest cavity and laying her eggs.

In the glow of red light, turtle volunteers help gather information about the number of eggs.

not sure why female leatherbacks don't move farther up the beach and lessen the chance of their eggs becoming inundated with seawater. Perhaps as the largest sea turtles on the planet, with many females weighing from five hundred pounds to more than a thousand pounds, the turtle has decided it takes too much energy to move that bulk to higher ground.

Even in the dim light it's clear that this mother sea turtle is the worse for wear. The smooth black leatherlike carapace is covered with deep cuts and scratches. She is missing half of her right rear flipper. There is a nasty gash on her "shoulder," where the front flipper meets the shell.

"This is a young mother. She is not that big. She's tagged already," says Kimberly. "Many of these cuts are mating wounds. Males can be twice the size of females and clasp the female by its leathery shell during mating. Some of these cuts are also from fishing line, and she probably lost her rear flipper to a shark bite." Kimberly speaks softly, never taking her eyes off the mother leatherback. Everyone puts on latex surgical gloves. One of the young girls, Zidane, gently moves sand away from the edge of the nesting hole and inches closer.

Kimberly peers into the nest cavity. It has begun to fill with water.

"Let's back away and give her some room," says Kimberly. "Hopefully she will relocate to higher ground."

After a few more attempts to dig out the sopping sand, the female stops, abandons the nest, and lumbers forward a few feet. She is only three feet from the first hole when she begins digging a second one. The group crouches behind her again and looks on like anxious family members at a birth. There is no wind. Over the steady rhythm of breaking waves, they hear the labored breathing of the leatherback in surprisingly loud sighs.

The sea turtle has been out of the water for a little over an hour, and her egg laying is a long way from completion. Most leatherbacks take an hour to an hour and a half for the whole process — to select a site, excavate a nest, lay eggs, camouflage the site, and return to the ocean. On land and away from the buoyancy of the water, the turtle's internal

The carapace of this female leatherback shows scars. These marks may have been left by the males, which can be twice as big as females, or may be the result of run-ins with fishing hooks, nets, boat strikes, or sharks.

TURTLE-WATCHING TOOLKIT

When most folks are digesting dinner and thinking about bedtime, turtle watchers are packing for work. What does a turtle watcher need for a night out on the beach? Well, if you're Dr. Kimberly Stewart, it's a lot of coffee, an energy bar, a large bag with assorted equipment, and a box, much like a fishing tackle box.

Kimberly hopes the color of her lime green clipboard stands out if it's ever lost on the beach.

Kimberly has everything she needs for her nightly turtle watch with her tackle box and bag.

In the bag:

1. A clipboard with sea turtle data sheets
2. Pencil or pen
3. Measuring tape for the nest location
4. Handheld GPS to record location coordinates for each nesting event
5. Stakes and flagging to mark the location of the nest
6. Cloth laundry bags to relocate eggs if needed
7. PIT (passive integrated transponder) tag reader
8. Cooler of ice to chill tissue or blood samples

And in the box:

1. Flexible measuring tape (large enough for a leatherback!)
2. Assortment of syringes, ranging in size from 3 ml to 12 ml
3. Needles, usually 1-inch, 22-gauge
4. PIT tags (tiny, glass-encased identification tags placed just under the skin)
5. PIT tag applicator
6. Tissue glue (to close the skin where the PIT tag is placed)
7. Dry gauze
8. Gauze soaked in antiseptic scrub and alcohol (to clean and disinfect prior to venipuncture or PIT tag placement)
9. Flipper tags, soaked in alcohol
10. Flipper tag applicators (similar to pliers)
11. Hawksbill and green sea turtle flipper tag applicator
12. Specimen cups
13. Selection of rubber gloves (sizes S-M-L-XL)
14. Sodium heparin (used to coat the syringes prior to blood collections)
15. Lithium heparin blood-collection tubes
16. Assortment of fine-point permanent markers (for writing on tubes, swabs, etc.)

organs feel the weight of the carapace. It is harder for them to breathe.

Kimberly checks in on the mother leatherback. The turtle seems clearly exhausted. Her breathing comes out in ragged gushes. The sand at the bottom of the nesting cavity is once again damp and collapsing.

"Leave her be for a bit," says Kimberly. "Sea turtles will come up to nest but sometimes it doesn't work out. They'll often try again the same night in a different location or try again the following night."

The mother leatherback suddenly stops her digging and pitches forward once more. This time she plows and plods a good distance higher up the beach. The family from St. Kitts looks on, almost willing the mother sea turtle to find a suitable spot. A deep exhalation accompanies every lurch the turtle makes. She finally settles in a place at least ten feet from the last nest hole. She begins twisting side to side and flinging sand with three-foot-long front flippers. This is her third time digging a body pit. The mother sea turtle pauses after each one or two lobs of sand.

The small group of midnight watchers huddle in a tight knot behind the mother leatherback to watch.

"She's begun digging her nest cavity," whispers Kimberly, crawling up behind the turtle.

The mother leatherback is using her rear flippers to shovel out sand. But her right

A leatherback female uses her wide, base-ball-glove–sized flippers to throw sand.

rear flipper, which ends in a ragged tear, has reached as far as it can go.

A nesting turtle is almost robotic in its movements. The left flipper extracts a cupful of sand, pats it to the side, and rests. Then the right flipper extracts a cupful of sand, pats it to the side, and rests. In this case, the mother sea turtle's right flipper is falling behind the left flipper. Kimberly steps in. In the brief two-second pause between the left flipper patting the sand and resting and before the right flipper begins to dig, Kimberly reaches in and scrapes out a fistful of sand. Eventually, with a little help from a friend, the mother leatherback is done. She can begin to lay her eggs.

Kimberly's experience tells her that despite the mother turtle's best efforts, the nest site could get inundated at high tide. The eggs will have to be relocated to a beach zone of lower

The mother turtle lays her eggs in a sandy cavity.

risk. Kimberly quickly spreads a sack into the nest hole just as the first eggs begin to fall.

"Stanley, can you hold her flipper back? And Zidane, can you count the eggs?" asks Kimberly.

"Sure," says Stanley.

"Okay," replies Zidane, lying prone, her cheek in the sand, her eyes on the white eggs falling from the mother turtle. "Four, so far."

"I'm going to check out her cuts," says Kimberly. She will record the severity of them, too.

Kimberly says there is really nothing she can do in a field setting to care for wounds. For there to be real benefit, the animal would need to be confined and started on antibiotics.

"The salt in ocean water is an antibacterial agent and is good for cuts and grazes," says Kimberly. "That's why dentists sometimes suggest you rinse your mouth with warm salty water after an extraction. Seawater will help clean and heal these wounds. It's the best we can do in this setting."

"Ninety-seven," say Stanley and Zidane in unison.

"Look! Now she's laying the small eggs," says Zidane.

"Those are the yolkless eggs. We'll count those, too," says Kimberly.

At about two a.m., Zidane is doing her best to concentrate. The wind has completely died and the sand gnats are taking advantage. After every count, she buries her face in her arms to dislodge the gnats. Stanley is providing good backup and double-checks Zidane's egg count.

"I think she is done," says Kimberly, leaning in, her headlamp illuminating a glistening pile of white sea turtle eggs. "How did she do?"

"Ninety-seven yolked and twenty-eight yolkless eggs," says Stanley.

"We counted every single one," adds Zidane proudly.

Kimberly and Stanley reach in to remove the egg sack. And just in time, too.

The leatherback's motionless egg-laying position is replaced with an intense bout of body shifts. Back flippers grab and push sand into the hole. The leatherback uses her front flippers to pivot her massive body in short jerks.

We back away and let the mother turtle complete her work. She is engaged in the serious job of camouflaging her nest. We have a job to do, too. We very gently haul the sack of eggs a further ten feet away from the water to a secure location.

"This is good. They'll be safe here," says Kimberly. "Who wants to dig?"

Zidane and her sister, Kimi-Lee, rally despite the early hour of the morning. They dive to the ground to dig. Within minutes, the new nest cavity is dug to the same depth and width as the original cavity. The family takes turns playing

Kimberly and her two young assistants, Zidane and Kimi-Lee, keep watchful eyes on the progress of the young mother turtle.

Kimberly shows Zidane and Kimi-Lee the pink spot, also known as the pineal spot, on the top of the leatherback's head. This spot is a unique indentifier for individual leatherbacks, much as our fingerprint is an identifier. Scientists believe the pink spot is related to the turtle's navigational ability.

mother sea turtle and each places some eggs into the hole. Once the eggs are tucked safely inside and covered, Kimberly marks the nest with a stick.

"Time to go," says Stanley, checking his watch. "You girls have a piano lesson and soccer practice in the morning."

Neither child wants to leave yet. Tessa and the girls walk back to the mother sea turtle and hunker down to watch her progress. She has spun completely around and is plodding back to the sea. The turtle watchers don't budge until the waves crest the mother leatherback's shell, the Caribbean Sea swallows her up again, and she is gone.

Dusk gathers on North Friars Beach on the east coast of St. Kitts. The beach is about a mile long.

A mother leatherback disappears back to the sea after leaving her clutch of eggs in a cavity along the high-tide line.

CHAPTER 8

SAVING SEA TURTLES

No one knows better than Kimberly that the island and its turtles are confronted with many challenges. But getting families like the Knights involved and helping to spread the message of sea turtle conservation gives Kimberly great hope.

"Even though I have worked with the sea turtles on St. Kitts for more than a decade, there is no letting up. Just last week two men began building a beach shack at the end of Keys Beach. I found them one morning nailing pieces of rough, weather-beaten plywood together. They had three walls up and were working on the roof. They wanted to turn it into a beach bar. And this was smack dab in the middle of prime nesting habitat. The entrepreneurial spirit is admirable, and

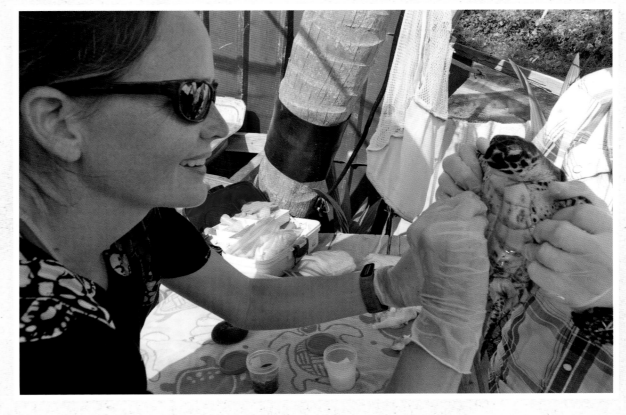

Kimberly cleans a young hawksbill, one of the turtles she is helping to rehabilitate on St. Kitts.

everybody loves a party. But the bar would have brought loud nighttime music, lights, crowds, and traffic. The nesting beach would have been ruined." Kimberly alerted a conservation officer who confronted them.

"They don't own the land, and have thirty days to remove the building," she says. "I hope they do. In 2011, the whole area was designated a biosphere reserve by the United Nations Educational, Scientific and Cultural Organization [UNESCO]. It is called St. Mary's Biosphere Reserve. It's the first biosphere reserve in the English-speaking Caribbean. UNESCO appointed me coordinator of the reserve. The reserve itself is very large and includes cloud forests in the mountains to the ocean shore and coral reefs. And while Keys Beach is only a small part of the reserve, thank goodness it is included.

"You know there are still people living right next door to the nesting beaches who have no idea that sea turtles nest in their backyard? This is why education and public outreach campaigns are key. If people are not aware of

Kimberly and a turtle volunteer check out the activity at Keys Beach, a leatherback nesting site.

Ecotourism is helping to make sea turtle hatchlings an attraction rather than a target.

how much the sea turtles depend on these increasingly scarce sandy beaches at the edge of the sea, how will they know what precautions to take to protect them or how urgent the need is?"

Kimberly often emphasizes that the future of this small colony of sea turtles, living legends from the Age of Dinosaurs, depends on stronger legal protection for the turtles and their main nesting beaches, as well as on the construction of a public sea turtle interpretive center at Keys Beach. The center would give sea turtle conservation a home and go a long way toward enabling full sustainability and community engagement. Protection

Opposite: Kimberly educates five young boys about St. Kitts's sea turtles.

"Students from the Ross University Preparatory School make calendars each year with photos, then sell them all around the island and all of the proceeds go to the SKSTMN," says Kimberly. "Each year they present me with a check. It helps a lot with paying salaries for the fishermen."

efforts can succeed only if people are willing to let the turtles live. In St. Kitts, as in so many other Caribbean countries, that can be achieved only if alternative sources of income — like the jewelry-making venture — are available and people are able to take advantage of them.

Kimberly remains hopeful that a community consensus — as well as a national consensus — can be reached on behalf of these gentle creatures. The sea turtle conservation program is supported by government, hotels, community groups, students, and even foreign volunteers. And its association with WIDECAST ensures that the work done here contributes to, and draws inspiration from, sea turtle research and conservation projects elsewhere throughout the Caribbean region.

"Turtle science is a work in progress and sometimes the progress is slow," says Kimberly. "But we don't let up. Our studies and work on nesting leatherbacks will continue." With luck, more and more turtles will return every year to their birth beaches in St. Kitts to successfully produce the next generation of sea turtles. And with each decision to let a sea turtle live, volunteer on the night patrols, help pick up litter and debris from coastal areas, and lobby government for stronger regulations, Kittitians are setting an example for other Caribbean islands to follow.

One Kittitian, in particular, is doing his part to set an example for the younger generation. "Do you know a sea turtle can carry a message on its back around the world?" says Theophilus Taylor, this time as he attaches a satellite transmitter onto the carapace of a rare hawksbill sea turtle. A smile as wide as the open ocean lights Theo's face.

Theo knows that this one small deed on this one small beach can be a part of something greater. Like a stone thrown into a quiet bay, one action will ripple far and wide, broadcasting a message of hope for the survival of these ancient creatures. The work Theo does with Kimberly (and the work of others like them) in all the small, quiet places ensures that the message of turtle conservation keeps traveling around the world.

GLOSSARY

ADULT: At full size and strength; sexually mature.

BASKING: A behavior that exposes the body, or a portion of the body, to the warmth of the sun.

BODY PIT: A depression the female sea turtle makes above the high-tide line before she digs a hole to lay her eggs. The body pit removes the dry surface from the nesting site.

CALIPEE: Sea turtle cartilage cut from the bones of the bottom of the sea turtle shell; traditionally stewed with turtle meat to make soup.

CARAPACE: A bony shield or shell covering the back (top) of a sea turtle.

CARNIVORE: An animal that preys (feeds) on other animals; a meat eater.

CARUNCLE: A temporary "egg tooth" (located on the hatchling's nose) used to break open the eggshell.

CENTIMETER: A metric unit of length, equal to one hundredth of a meter. One meter equals 100 centimeters (about 39.37 inches); a centimeter measures about 3/8 inch.

CITES: Convention on International Trade in Endangered Species.

CLUTCH: The number of eggs laid by a turtle at one time.

COUNTER-SHADING: A form of camouflage where an animal is darker on top and lighter on the bottom.

DRIFT LINES: Elongated masses of seaweed, debris, and other floating objects that often form where ocean currents converge (meet one another).

ECTOTHERM: An animal that is dependent on external sources of body heat (scientists used to call this "cold-blooded").

EGG CHAMBER: A hole dug by an adult female turtle using her rear flippers, into which she lays her eggs.

ENDANGERED SPECIES: Under the U.S. Endangered Species Act, "Any species which is in danger of extinction throughout all or a significant portion of its range."

FERTILE: An egg capable of producing a viable embryo.

FLIPPER: A broad, flat limb used for swimming or digging.

FLIPPER TAG: A uniquely numbered metal or plastic tag to mark sea turtles.

GPS (GLOBAL POSITIONING SYSTEM): An accurate worldwide navigational facility based on satellite reception.

HATCHLING: A newly hatched turtle.

INCUBATION: Maintaining eggs at the most favorable temperature so they develop and hatch.

KITTITIAN: A person from the island of St. Kitts in the eastern Caribbean Sea.

LACRIMAL GLAND: Salt gland that assists in the regulation of salt in the sea turtle's body, preventing it from becoming dehydrated by shedding salty tears.

Kimberly holds a green sea turtle up for a view of its plastron.

MUTUALISM: Teamwork that is vital to survival.

NATAL BEACH HOMING: The ability of an adult sea turtle to return to her birthplace (natal beach) to lay her eggs.

NECROPSY: The autopsy of a dead animal.

PELAGIC: Relating to or living in the open ocean; an organism that lives in open seas.

PINK SPOT: The unpigmented splotch on the crown (top) of a leatherback sea turtle's head; may aid in navigation by giving the turtle a mechanism to measure day length.

PIT TAG: Passive integrated transponder tag. PIT tags are small, inert microprocessors sealed in glass that can transmit a unique identification number to a handheld reader when the reader briefly activates the tag with a low-frequency radio signal at close range. A PIT tag is cylindrical, about the size of a grain of rice, and is injected under the skin or into the muscle.

PLANKTON: Microscopic organisms drifting or floating in the ocean. They supply an important source of food to many large marine animals, such as fish and whales.

PLASTRON: The bottom portion of a turtle's shell.

PREDATOR: An animal that hunts and eats other animals.

SARGASSO SEA: A vast area of nearly motionless water in the central basin of the north Atlantic Ocean, named for the sargassum (or gulfweed) that floats on the surface.

YOLKED EGG: An egg capable of becoming a new sea turtle.

YOLKLESS EGG: An egg that will not produce young because it contains no yolk.

Adapted from David Gulko and Karen Eckert, *Sea Turtles: An Ecological Guide* (Honolulu: Mutual Publishing, 2004).

HOW TO HELP SEA TURTLES

Join a sea turtle organization such as WIDECAST or St. Kitts Sea Turtle Monitoring Network. Visit them on the Web at www.widecast.org or www.stkittsturtles.org.

1. Carry a reusable bag when you or your parents go shopping. Let the store clerk know that you're concerned about single-use plastic bags, and encourage the store to sell durable shopping bags and to offer incentives to customers who use them.
2. Advocate for ocean conservation and always buy sustainably harvested seafood. Certain fishing methods can harm sea turtles. Longline fishing intended to catch open-ocean fish, such as tuna and swordfish, often snag sea turtles, sharks, and seabirds. Visit the Monterey Bay Aquarium Seafood Watch website to learn about ocean-friendly seafood choices: www.montereybay-aquarium.org/cr/seafoodwatch.aspx.

HOW TO ADOPT A SEA TURTLE

Kimberly says, "There are two ways to adopt a sea turtle. You can adopt a nesting turtle or you can adopt a rehabilitation patient. Either way, you get a certificate with a photo of your adopted turtle along with information about sea turtles and the St. Kitts Sea Turtle Monitoring Network."

It costs about fifty dollars to adopt a turtle and it is a great way to support sea turtle conservation. You can learn all about sea turtle adoption by visiting www.stkittsturtles.org/www.stkittsturtles.org/Sea_Turtle_Adoption.html.

A batch of hawksbill hatchlings in hand.

WEBSITES TO ENJOY

Archelon (giant turtle of ancient seas) — Black Hills Institute of Geological Research   www.bhigr.com/pages/info/info_arch.htm

Euro Turtle
www.euroturtle.org

Florida Fish and Wildlife Conservation Commission — Sea Turtles   myfwc.com/wildlifehabitats/managed/sea-turtles

Florida Marine Research Institute — Light Pollution   www.fws.gov/caribbean/es/PDF/Library%20Items/LightingManual-Florida.pdf

Georgia Sea Turtle Center   www.georgiaseaturtl-ecenter.org

Monterey Bay Aquarium Seafood Watch www.montereybayaquarium.org/cr/seafood-watch.aspx

Sea Turtle Postage Stamps of the World www.2xtreme.net/~nlinsley

St. Catherines Island Sea Turtle Conservation Program   www.scistp.org

St. Kitts Sea Turtle Monitoring Network (Kimberly invites everyone to check out the St. Kitts sea turtle website, join the network's Facebook page, adopt a sea turtle, and learn more about the exciting plans for a sea turtle interpretive center.) www.stkittsturtles.org

The Ocean Conservancy — International Coastal Cleanup Day   www.oceanconservancy.org

U.S. Fish and Wildlife Service — Sea Turtles www.fws.gov/northflorida/SeaTurtles/seaturtle-info.htm

U.S. National Marine Fisheries Service — Sea Turtles   www.nmfs.noaa.gov/pr/species/turtles

WIDECAST — Wider Caribbean Sea Turtle Conservation Network   www.widecast.org

WIDECAST — Basic Sea Turtle Biology www.widecast.org/Biology/BasicBiology.html

WIDECAST — Threats to Sea Turtle Survival www.widecast.org/Conservation/Threats.html

World Wildlife Fund — Climate Change and Sea Turtles   wwf.panda.org/what_we_do/endangered_species/marine_turtles/lac_marine_turtle_programme/projects/climate_turtles

BOOKS TO ENJOY

FOR YOUNGER READERS

Davies, Nicola. *One Tiny Turtle: Read and Wonder.* Illustrated by Jane Chapman. New York: Candlewick Press, 2005.

Marsh, Laura. *National Geographic Readers: Sea Turtles.* Washington, D.C.: National Geographic Society, 2011.

Monroe, Mary Alice, and Barbara J. Bergwert. *Turtle Summer: A Journal for My Daughter.* Mt. Pleasant, S.C.: Sylvan Dell Publishing, 2007.

Pirotta, Saviour, and Nilesh Mistry. *Turtle Bay.* New York: Farrar, Straus and Giroux, 1997.

Rhodes, Mary Jo. *Sea Turtles (Undersea Encounters).* Photographs by David Hall. Danbury, Conn.: Children's Press, 2005.

Stevenson, Andrew. *The Turtle Who Ate a Balloon.* Flatts, Bermuda: Bermuda Zoological Society, 2007.

Swinburne, Stephen R. *Turtle Tide: The Ways of Sea Turtles.* Illustrated by Bruce Hiscock. Honesdale, Pa.: Boyds Mills Press, 2005.

Tara, Stephanie Lisa. *I'll Follow the Moon.* Illustrated by Lee Edward Fodi. Dallas: Brown Books Publishing Group, 2005.

Yee, Tammy. *Baby Honu's Incredible Journey.* Waipahu, Hawaii: Island Heritage Press, 1997.

FOR OLDER READERS

Carr, Archie. *So Excellent a Fishe: A Natural History of Sea Turtles*. Garden City, N.Y.: The Natural History Press, 1967.

———. *The Windward Road: Adventures of a Naturalist on Remote Caribbean Shores*. Gainesville: University Press of Florida, 1979.

Devaux, Bernard, and Bernard de Wetter. *On the Trail of Sea Turtles*. Paris: Barron's Nature Travel Guides, 2000.

Gulko, David, and Karen Eckert. *Sea Turtles: An Ecological Guide*. Honolulu, Hawaii: Mutual Publishing, 2004.

Perrine, Doug. *Sea Turtles of the World*. Stillwater, Minn.: Voyageur Press, 2003.

Ripple, Jeff. *Sea Turtles*. WorldLife Library. Stillwater, Minn.: Voyageur Press, 1996.

Safina, Carl. *Voyage of the Turtle: In Pursuit of the Earth's Last Dinosaur*. New York: Henry Holt & Co., 2006.

Watt, E. Melanie. *Leatherback Turtles*. Austin, Tex.: Raintree Steck-Vaughn Publishers, 2002.

ACKNOWLEDGMENTS

Special thanks to Dr. Kimberly Stewart at the St. Kitts Sea Turtle Monitoring Network and Dr. Karen Eckert at WIDECAST. I could not have written this book without them. I am grateful to Dr. Scott Eckert at Principia College and to Theophilus Taylor in St. Kitts. I would also like to thank Stanley, Tessa, Kimi-Lee, and Zidane Knight, Kate Walsh, George Stiegler, Gary Buckles, Jeremy M. McKeever, and Jon Romano. And many thanks to my nephew, Sasha Spassoff, a trusty assistant.

I am very grateful for the many wonderful photographs that appear in this book. A big thank-you to all the photographers who kindly donated their images.

My two wonderful editors, Cynthia Platt and Erica Zappy, provided direction and support. I'm grateful for their steadfast editorial guidance throughout the writing of *Sea Turtle Scientist*.

PHOTO CREDITS

INDEX

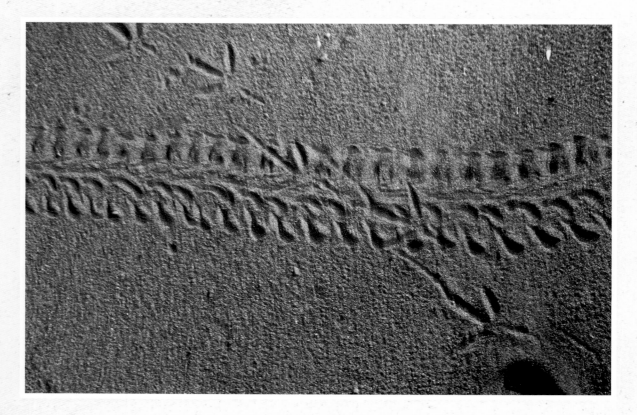

SCIENTISTS IN THE FIELD
WHERE SCIENCE MEETS ADVENTURE

Check out these titles to meet more scientists who are out in the field—
and contributing every day to our knowledge of the world around us:

 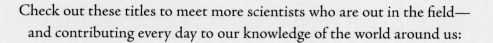    

 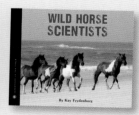    

  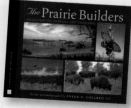    

Looking for even more adventure? Craving updates on the work of your favorite scientists, as well as in-depth video
footage, audio, photography, and more? Then visit the new Scientists in the Field website!

WWW.SCIENCEMEETSADVENTURE.COM